Small Tunes

for

Young Harpists

By Bonnie Goodrich

Bel Artes Publishing, 4407 Verone, Bellaire, TX 77401

First Piece

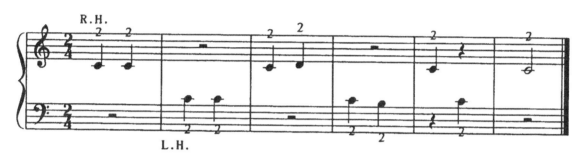

Lots of C's

Visiting Miami

Scales in 4/4

Nicky's Harp Piece

Playing on the Lawn

Trip to Spain

Waltz in A Minor

Turquoise Dress

Scales for Hobbes

Etude for Placing

Ginger's Etude

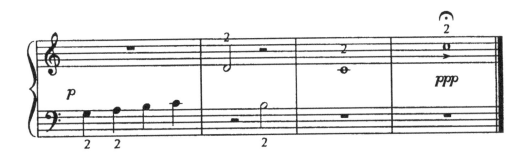

Second Etude with Brackets

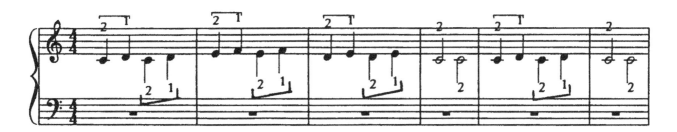

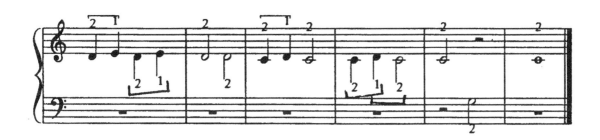

Summertime

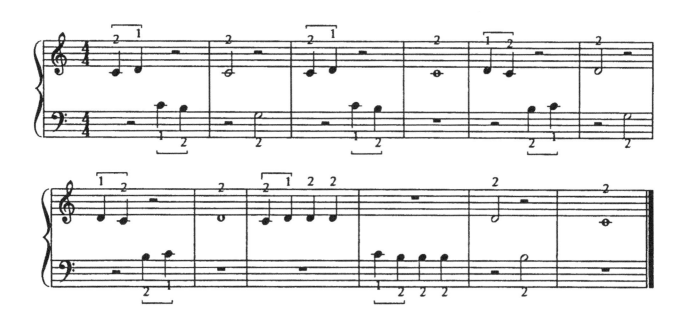

8

Red Bows

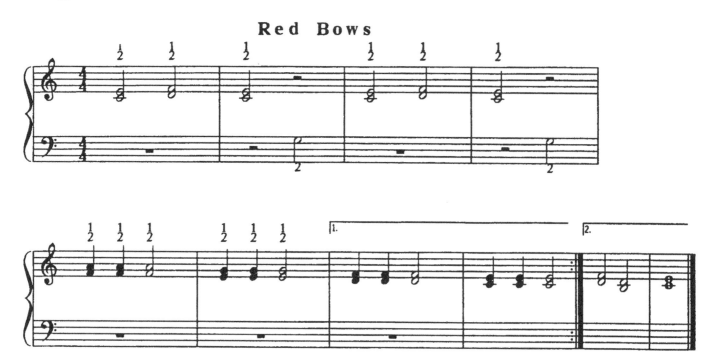

Ginger in the Grass

March of Bill the Cat

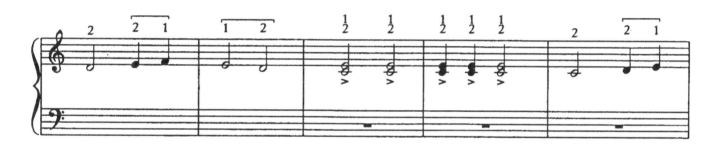

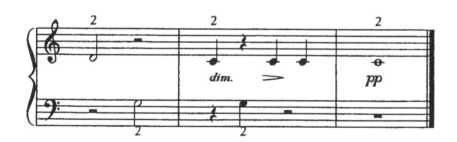

April Dance

Neighbors of C

Placing Finger Three

3-2-1, 1-2-3

Ballet Class

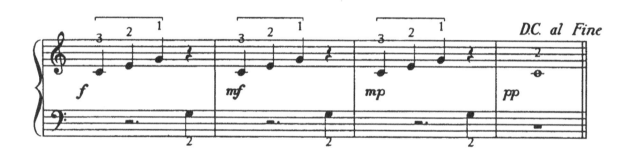

Summer Shade

Harp Movers' March

A Very Small Harp

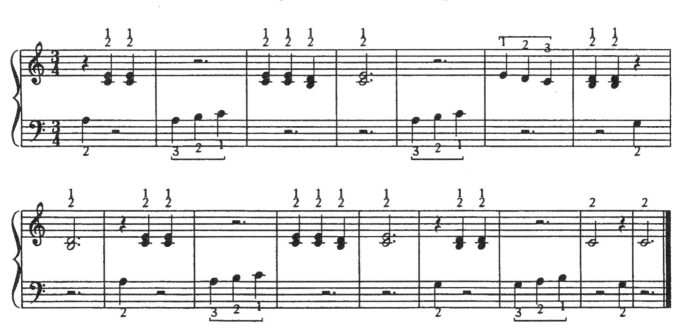

Waltz for an Antique Harp

Gracefully
(Bring out R.H. melody)

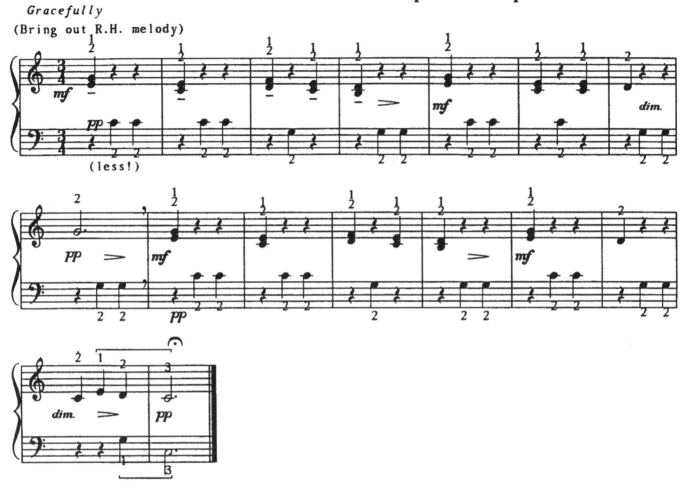

More Brackets with 3's

The Ice-Cream Waltz

With a Lilt

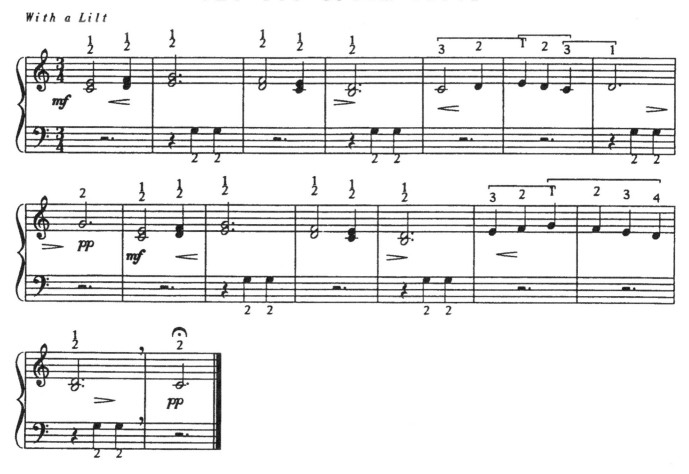

Swimming

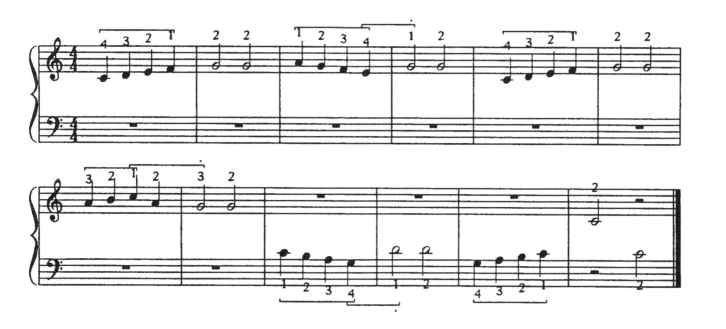

Dragonfly

Frere Jacques

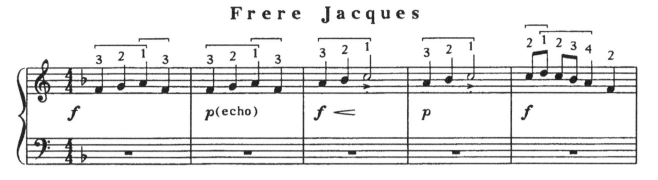

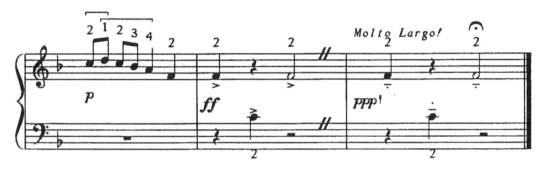

The Spaces Spell "Face"!

C—Major Etude

Calico Cats

Dancing Dinosaurs

Make 2 G♯'s

The Catnip Waltz

Playfully
(Bring out L.H. melody!)

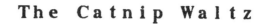

L.H. very legato

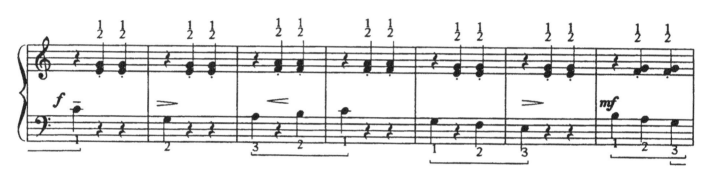

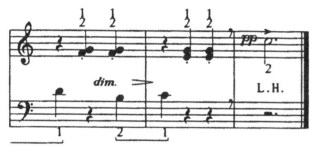

Hiccups

Marching to Camp
(Drill on the Spaces)

Z–Jig/Brian Boru's March

Sneezing Rabbits

A Medieval Tale

Gypsy Moth

Rain Dance for Frogs

Climbing Trees!

Flight of the Swallow

Popcorn

L.H. muffles R.H. notes
very quickly with flat hand

L.H. continues thru rest of piece...

rit.

(R.H.)

sfz!
very
abrupt!

Spanish Lament

Clare the Cat

Lullaby for a Young Squirrel

Doo-Dad

Broccoli

Minuet for Water Bugs

* With the R.H., slide a metal rod or the shaft of a tuning key rapidly down the indicated string immediately after plucking with the L.H. to produce a water-drop sound!